Make it with

Fabric

BOOK HOUSE

Published in Great Britain in 2003 by Book House, an imprint of
The Salariya Book Company Ltd
25 Marlborough Place, Brighton BN1 1UB

Please visit the Salariya Book Company at:
www.salariya.com
www.book-house.co.uk

ISBN 1 904194 86 9

A catalogue record for this book is available from the British Library.

Printed and bound in Spain.

Contents

Introduction

Introduction

Introduction

Look around carefully and you will see that fabrics are a part of almost every area of our daily lives. The art of weaving is very old. It basically consists of interweaving several pieces of thread alternately and regularly until a solid sheet or panel has been created. In the old days, only natural fibres were used. But now thousands of artificial or synthetic fabrics (fabrics made from materials not found in nature, such as nylon) are also used.

You can create new and original objects from different types of fabrics. To make the craft projects that we show you here you will not have to cut up dresses and outfits. You will find scraps of fabric, old clothing, wool, cleaning cloths, old rags, socks and other things to make the projects. See for yourself how you will be able to make a variety of things with these materials that are fun and that will be useful at the same time: a pillow to keep your pyjamas in, or a sock puppet to amuse your friends.

Commonly found natural and synthetic fabrics have been used to make the craft projects listed in this book. Some of the projects will serve as a very basic introduction to the world of sewing. All you need is a large size needle and a little skill to work it through the fabric.

In order to make these craft projects, you will need to have a number of items that you should be able to find at home (scissors, large size needle, glue) and you will have to follow the steps carefully. Also, you will find that you can achieve different results by making slight changes. We suggest some ideas to help you do so.

REMEMBER! Whenever you see the symbol below, or when you are using scissors, ask an adult to help you.

Bird Bird Bird

Bird

Let's make a beautiful bird from a simple sponge cloth.
Follow these steps carefully.

You will need:
- scissors
- glue stick
- red felt-tip pen
- yellow wool
- yellow sponge cloth
- green sponge cloth
- black felt

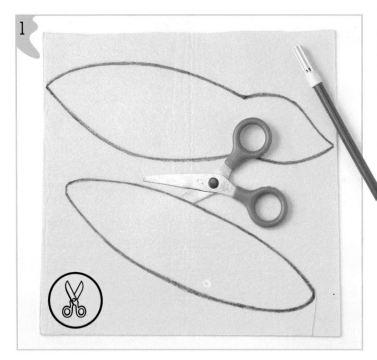

1 With a red felt-tip pen draw the outlines of the body and the wings on a yellow sponge cloth and cut them out.

2 Make a slit in the bird's body, which will later be used to insert the wing.

3 Draw and cut out the tail, the beak and the eyes of the bird on a green sponge cloth. Remember to make two of each piece.

4 Glue the tail, the beak and the eyes to each side of the bird's body.

5 Cut out the pupils from the black felt and glue them on the eyes. Make a little hole on the back of the bird and thread a piece of yellow wool through it for hanging.

Insert the wing in the slit that you made before and the bird is completed. As you can see, the sponge cloth has been transformed into a happy bird.

Let your imagination soar

Other ideas:
By practically following the same steps you can make an aeroplane...

House Shoe-Bag

Would you like to put away your shoes in an original and fun way? Follow these directions carefully to make your house shoe-bag.

Toolbox

You will need:
- scissors
- red, green and yellow thread
- a large-eyed needle
- brown, red, yellow and green linen or similar fabric

1 To make the roof, cut out a piece of red fabric in the shape of a triangle. Then for the front of the house, cut out a rectangle from a piece of brown fabric. The short sides should measure the same as the base of the roof.

2 Attach the roof to the front of the house with red thread and a large-eyed needle.

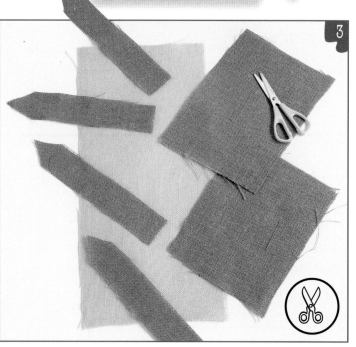

3 Cut out two rectangles from a piece of green fabric for the windows. Then cut a rectangle from a piece of yellow fabric the same length as the front of the house and wide enough to hold your shoes. Finally, cut out four strips of green fabric to make a fence.

8

4 Using yellow thread and a large-eyed needle, attach the two windows to the front of the house, leaving the top part unsewn.

5 Sew the yellow rectangle to the front of the house along the bottom. Finally, sew on the four green strips, the two middle ones on each side of the centre to separate the three pockets.

Let your imagination soar

Other ideas:
You can invent any shape for the shoe-bag: a train, a kangaroo, a tree...

Braided Doll

You can give life to a skein of wool by creating a beautiful braided doll! To do it, follow these directions.

1 With the help of a friend make an oval ring with green wool and tie it on one of the sides with coloured wool. Then cut the ring on the opposite side.

2 Following the same procedure make another ring, but this one should be smaller and made with different coloured wool, which will be the hair. Put the two bunches together.

Toolbox

You will need:
- scissors
- white glue
- black felt
- one skein of green wool and another of mixed colours

3 Next, using coloured wool, tie a knot at approximately 5 cm below the hair. Now you have the doll's head.

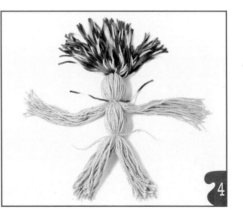

4 To make the arms, separate two bunches of wool and tie another knot with green wool at the height that would be the waist. Make the legs by separating the remaining wool into two more bunches.

5 Braid the arms and the legs and tie them at the ends.

6 Cut out two eyes from black felt and glue them onto the face of the doll. Finally, arrange the hair as you wish.

And there it is, the braided doll! It wasn't that difficult to give life to a simple skein of wool, was it?

Let your imagination soar

Other ideas:
Using only one skein of wool make the head, braid eight legs and you will have a fun octopus.

Ball

With only a few stockings or tights and polyester fibrefill you can make a great ball. To design it follow these directions.

Toolbox

You will need:
- scissors
- orange, white, red and blue stockings or tights
- polyester fibrefill

1 Cut off part of a red stocking below the knee.

2 Insert the fibrefill material through the opening until a very firm ball has been formed.

3 Cut off the leftover piece of stocking to make a round ball.

4 Pinch different parts of the white, blue and orange stockings and cut them to make holes.

5 Insert the ball into the white stocking and cut off the excess part of the stocking.

6 Follow the same procedure as in step 5 with the blue and orange stockings.

Have you seen how easy it is to make a ball? Now you can enjoy playing with it with your friends.

Let your imagination soar

Other ideas:
If you make all the holes the same size, using black and white stockings, the ball will look like a football.

Car with Trailer

With this entertaining craft project you will be able to add a new car model to your collection. To design it follow these steps.

1 Make a pattern of the car by drawing the outline on a piece of orange cardboard and then cutting it out.

Toolbox

You will need:
- scissors
- large-eyed needle
- red felt-tip pen
- white glue
- green sponge cloth
- orange sponge cloth
- red wool
- black felt
- orange felt
- 2 sheets of thin orange cardboard

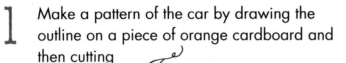

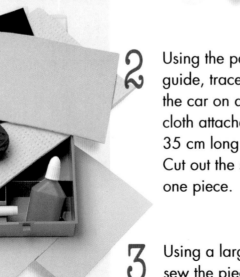

2 Using the pattern as a guide, trace two outlines of the car on a green sponge cloth attached to a strip 35 cm long and 6 cm wide. Cut out the shape in one piece.

3 Using a large-eyed needle sew the piece with red wool.

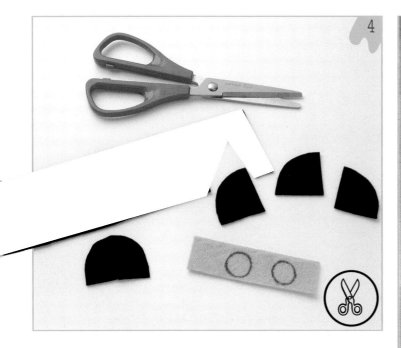

4 Draw five windows, four for the sides and one for the front, on a piece of black felt. Draw two headlights on a piece of orange felt and cut everything out.

5 Glue all these pieces to their proper places on the car.

6 To make the wheels, cut out four strips of orange felt 25 cm long by 1.5 cm wide, and four strips of black felt 20 cm long by 1.5 cm wide. Place the black felt on top of the orange one and roll them together. Glue the end with white glue.

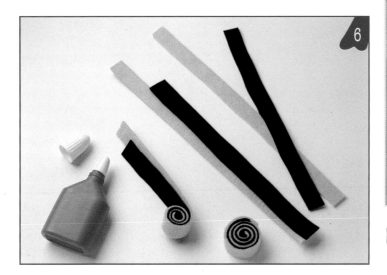

7 Glue the four wheels onto the car with white glue.

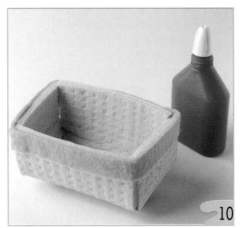

8 Draw the pattern of the trailer on orange cardboard. The base should be approximately 8 cm long by 5 cm wide and the sides 4 cm high. Cut out the shape.

9 Trace the pattern of the trailer onto a piece of green sponge cloth and cut it out.

10 Cut out a strip of orange felt 26 cm long by 1 cm wide and use it to hold the four sides of the trailer together by glueing it with white glue.

11 Following step 7, make the two wheels for the trailer. In this case the strips should be shorter so the wheels can be smaller, and the orange strip will go over the black one.

16

12 With a large-eyed needle make a hole in the rear of the car and another one in the front of the trailer. String a piece of red wool through these two holes and make a knot at each end.

Put your favourite toy figure in the trailer and take it for a ride around the world!

Let your imagination soar

Other ideas:
You can add as many accessories to your car as you want, for example, a registration number, a radio aerial...

Sock Puppet

Sock Puppet
Sock Puppet
Sock Puppet

Make a sock come to life by turning it into a playful puppet. Follow these steps to make your puppet.

1 Make a cut near the toe of the sock. This cut should be approximately 3 cm long.

Toolbox

You will need:
- one sock
- scissors
- red thread
- needle (normal size)
- red felt
- black felt
- cotton-wool balls
- double-sided tape

2 Cut out an oval, about 8 cm long, from a piece of red felt.

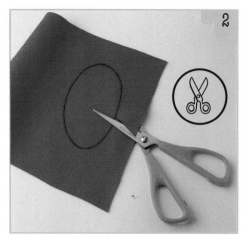

3 Turn the sock inside out and sew the red oval over the opening that you have previously made. Now you have the puppet's mouth.

4 Cut out eyes from a piece of black felt and glue them onto two cotton-wool balls

Ask your friends to create a sock puppet of their own and entertain people with your wonderful characters!

5 Finally, attach the cotton-wool balls with double-sided tape above the mouth of the puppet, opposite the heel.

Let your imagination soar

Other ideas:
You can give your puppet wonderful hairstyles by adding different coloured wool.

Organiser

With this fun and easy craft project you can make a great organiser for your pencils. To design it, follow these steps carefully.

Toolbox

You will need:
- scissors
- stapler
- piece of string or shoelace 70 cm long
- yellow sponge cloth 40 cm by 40 cm
- green sponge cloth
- ruler
- black felt-tip pen

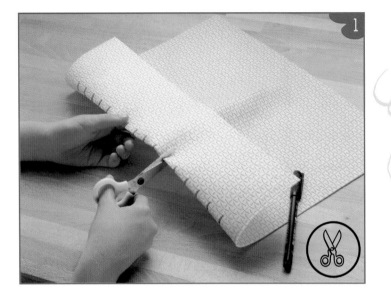

1 Make a fold 10 cm from one of the edges of the yellow sponge cloth and make 16 cuts of 1.5 cm each. Leave a 2 cm space between the cuts.

2 Cut a strip of green sponge cloth 1.5 cm wide by 45 cm long.

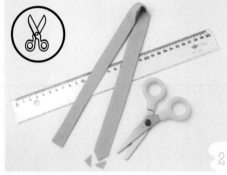

3 Weave the green strip through the cuts that you made before.

4 Staple the strip at the two edges of the sponge cloth.

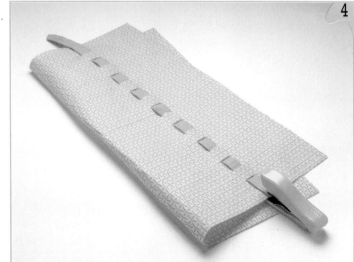

5 Now make two small holes at the end of the strip and insert the 70 cm-long string through them.

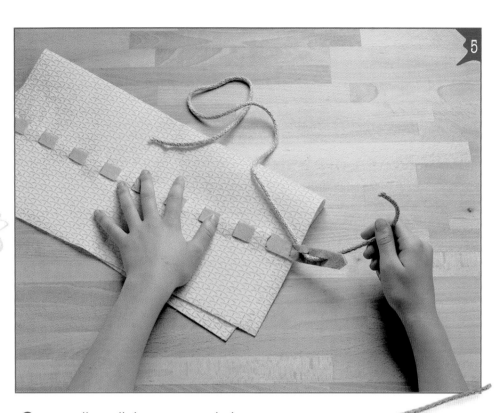

6 Finally, roll the sponge cloth and tie it with the string.

The organiser is finished! This is the most original and practical organiser you'll ever own!

Let your imagination soar

Other ideas:
If you make the cuts bigger and the spaces farther apart, you can use this organiser to hold anything you want.

Wool Bug

You can create a little best friend to take with you wherever you go. To make it, follow these steps carefully.

Wool Bug
Wool Bug
Wool Bug

Toolbox

You will need:
- scissors
- cardboard
- white glue
- wool in two shades of blue
- black felt-tip pen
- flesh-coloured felt
- black felt
- white felt

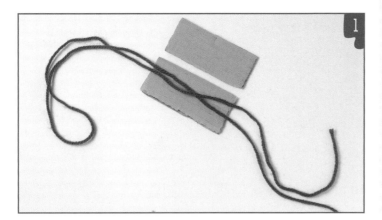

1   Cut out two pieces of cardboard 5 cm wide and 8 cm long. Then cut a piece of blue wool 40 cm long and put it, folded in half, between the two pieces of cardboard.

2   Wrap both shades of blue wool around the cardboard pieces. The more wool you wrap around, the puffier your ball will be.

3   Tie a knot with the two ends of the 40 cm piece of wool that hangs from either end of the cardboard.

4   Separate the cardboard pieces from the wool and cut it all the way around to make the ball.

22

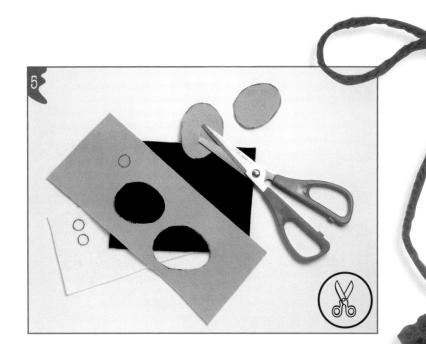

Here is your wool bug! Your new and loyal friend is ready to join you on any adventure.

5 Draw and cut out eyes (one white and one black) from two pieces of felt, then a nose and two feet from a flesh-coloured piece. Make a small hole in the centre of each foot with scissors.

6 Glue the eyes and the nose to the ball. Finally, thread each wool 'leg' through each foot and make a knot at any height you want.

Let your imagination soar

Other ideas:
You can make different colour bugs with different wools.
You can also change its size or make one without legs.

Pyjama Pillow

If you want to put away your pyjamas neatly and to be more comfortable than ever at the same time, design this original pyjama storage pillow. To make it, follow these steps carefully.

Toolbox

You will need:
- scissors
- green and yellow thread
- large-eyed needle
- fabric (red and yellow)
- polyester fibrefill

1 With a large-eyed needle and yellow thread sew two pieces of red cloth together on three sides only.

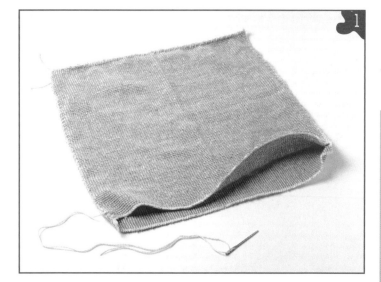

2 Insert the filling through the side that you have not sewn.

3 Close the pillow by sewing the open side with green thread.

4 To make the pocket, fold the yellow cloth in half and sew it with green thread.

There it is, your pyjama pillow! Do you know a more 'comfortable' way of storing your pyjamas?

Let your imagination soar

Other ideas:
You can make the pillow with different colours or make a flap to close the pocket.

Bookmark

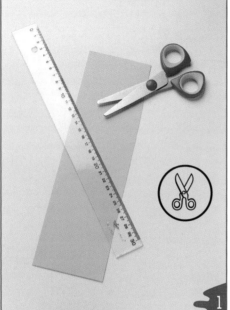

If you always want to remember the page where you last stopped reading, put together this bookmark. To make it, follow these directions step-by-step.

Bookmark

Toolbox

You will need:
- scissors
- black felt-tip pen
- glue stick
- denim fabric
- patterned fabric
- black felt
- flesh-coloured felt
- thin cardboard
- ruler

1 Cut out a strip of thin cardboard 25 cm long and 8 cm wide.

2 Draw a T-shirt on the patterned fabric and trousers on the denim fabric and then cut them out.

3 Cut out the hair and shoes from a piece of black felt, and a face from a piece of flesh-coloured felt.

4 Arrange and glue all the pieces of the body on the strip of thin cardboard.

5 Cut out the shape of the body and form the hands with scissors.

Now you have finished the project, your bookmark person will reach up to hold your place!

Let your imagination soar
Other ideas:
You can make the figure in various poses and dress it with fabrics of different types.

Caterpillar

Would you like to have a new friend? Then have fun creating this fluffy and friendly caterpillar. To make it, follow these steps carefully.

Toolbox

You will need:
- scissors
- large-eyed needle
- glue stick
- red stockings or tights
- red wool
- black felt
- white felt
- polyester fibrefill
- black felt-tip pen

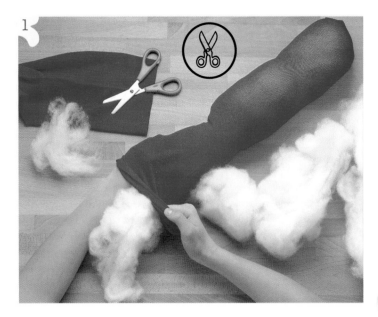

1   Cut off the stocking at the knee and insert the fibrefill material. Make a knot at the end.

2   Make the rings of the caterpillar by tying it with red wool. You will have to make six in all, five big ones and a smaller one for the nose.

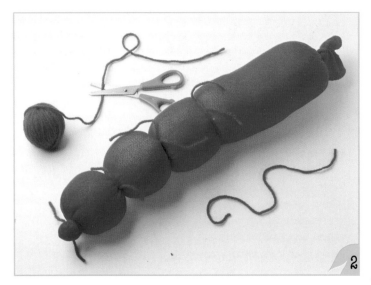

3   Cut out the eyes for the caterpillar from pieces of black and white felt. Then cut out four circles from black felt to make the spots.

4 Glue the eyes on the face and the spots all over the caterpillar's body.

5 Roll a piece of black felt and tie it with red wool to make the antennae.

6 Then sew the antennae to the head of the caterpillar with a large-eyed needle.

You have finished the caterpillar!
Isn't it easy to make new friends?

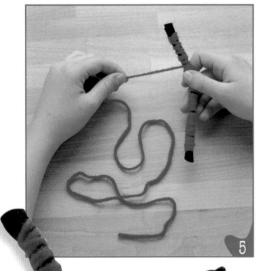

Let your imagination soar

Other ideas:
You can make different rings by using stockings of assorted colours or you can decorate the body of the caterpillar with other shapes.

29

Bag

Bag
Bag
Bag

With just a pair of scissors, felt and wool, you can put together a useful and colourful bag. To make it, follow the instructions step-by-step.

Toolbox

You will need:
- scissors
- black felt-tip pen
- blue felt
- yellow felt
- black wool
- ruler
- needle

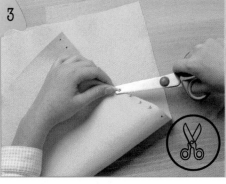

1   Cut out two strips of felt, one blue and one yellow, 25 cm wide. The blue one should be 70 cm long and the yellow one only 40 cm.

2   Make a small mark every 2 cm on both edges of the blue piece with a black marker. Repeat this procedure on the yellow piece.

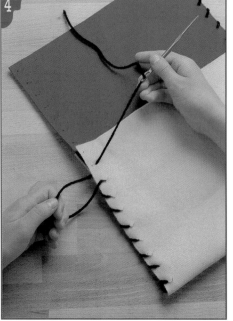

3   Make a small hole on each mark with the point of the scissors. To make this task easier, pinch together the border of the pieces of felt with your fingers.

4   Fold the piece of blue felt in half and the yellow one over it, and sew the edges with black wool.

5 Cut nine lengths of wool. Tie a knot at one end and make a braid.

6 Tie the braid to the two holes at the top of the bag.

Now you have a beautiful bag with three pockets to carry anything you want!

Let your imagination soar

Other ideas:
You can decorate the bag with different designs or glue new pockets on it.

Make it with
Fabrics

The fabrics used in this book are quite common, allowing children to learn to create using scraps that are found anywhere. Making craft projects with fabrics can introduce children to sewing techniques. Even so, the projects are designed to be assembled in different ways, without necessarily requiring the use of a needle and thread.

p.6   **Bird.** It is advisable for each child to create and draw his or her own bird in order to stimulate his or her creativity.
Ages 5 and up

p.8   **House Shoe-Bag.** To prevent the project from becoming monotonous, some parts of the house can be attached using double-sided tape.
Ages 7 and up

p.10   **Braided Doll.** For children 5 or 6 years of age, we suggest making the octopus instead because it is easier.
Ages 6 and up

p.12   **Ball.** Wool leggings can also be used instead of stocking material because they may be easier for younger children to manipulate.
Ages 5 and up

p.14   **Car with Trailer.** The most difficult part of this project is drawing the pattern, so an adult should help the children with this task.
Ages 7 and up

p.18   **Sock Puppet.** To make this project less complicated, the mouth can be stapled to the sock instead of sewn.
Ages 7 and up

p.20   **Organiser.** By substituting a button for the string, the child can be taught to do some basic sewing.
Ages 6 and up

p.22   **Wool Bug.** To make this project more creative, it is a good idea for the child to make several cotton-wool balls and then play at glueing them together to create his or her figure.
Ages 6 and up

p.24   **Pyjama Pillow.** Older children who already know how to sew can make the pillow with canvas or fabrics.
Ages 7 and up

p.26   **Bookmark.** To boost the interest of younger children, the theme of the bookmark can be related to one of his or her storybooks.
Ages 5 and up

p.28   **Caterpillar.** To make this a group project, we suggest making a long caterpillar by putting together several different stockings.
Ages 6 and up

p.30   **Bag.** For older children it is preferable to use felt for the strap of the bag, and to sew it at both ends to make it stronger.
Ages 7 and up